A Pastor's Journey
through Bereavement

A LIFE
A LIVED
WITH
LOVE

Norman Christie

In memory of my beloved wife,
Doreen.

Doreen Christie
26th September 1940 – 12th October 2016

A LIFE LIVED WITH LOVE
Copyright © 2021 by Norman Christie

ISBN 978-1-8382191-8-5

Main translation in use: NKJV

Emphasis within Scripture quotations is the author's own.

Published by
Maurice Wylie Media
Inspirational Christian Publisher

Publishers' statement: Throughout this book the love for our God is such that whenever we refer to Him we honour with Capitals. On the other hand, when referring to the devil, we refuse to acknowledge him with any honour to the point of violating grammatical rule and withholding capitalisation.

For more information visit
www.MauriceWylieMedia.com

Contents

Introduction

Since this is my first book, it is only fitting that I should introduce myself. Even those of you that know me personally, may not know my background story...

My father was called Richard Christie, a painting contractor, being part of the Christies' Wallpaper and Paints dynasty; well-known throughout Ulster. He was not only a successful businessman, but also for many years, an unpaid pastor in Bethesda Elim Church, Belfast. I was born in 1940, the youngest of his four sons. My three brothers entered the family painting business. However, I had no desire to follow their example, and in my teens, I decided to pursue a career in industrial chemistry.

Being conscious of God's call on my life to preach the gospel, I preached my first sermon at age 17 in Bethesda Elim, in Belfast. I became heavily involved in Sunday school, children and youth work for some 28 years. I met Doreen, the girl of my dreams, when we were both 18 years of age and got married in 1964. We were blessed with four wonderful children who went on to pursue a wide range of professional careers. Throughout their early childhoods, I continued to pursue a career in chemistry, finally obtaining a position in the local BP Oil Refinery, where I worked in the laboratory for 20 years approximately, becoming a Senior Technical Assistant. Nevertheless, I prayed virtually every day that I would enter the preaching ministry. The opportunity arose in 1982 when the Oil Refinery closed, and I was declared redundant.

I immediately applied for the ministry in the Elim Pentecostal Churches and was readily accepted at age 42 as a trainee pastor. My first church as a pastor was to Randalstown Elim Church. I then moved to South

Belfast Elim, and my last congregation, which I served for 19 years before retiring in 2011, was Lisburn Elim. Yet retirement does not mean one has stopped. I continue to preach and teach throughout the province in various denominations. I was not alone in the walk, as labouring alongside Doreen and my musically-gifted family was both pleasant and rewarding, but not without its trials.

When Doreen passed away in 2016, I was left alone; my three girls and son having married. Initially, I found bereavement devastatingly painful. I desperately needed to express my sense of utter grief and turned to the Lord in prayer. Living in His presence afforded me profound relief, and I felt strongly moved to write poems. This seemed to be strange guidance as I had not previously written poetry. I chose only to write when the pain was at its greatest and inspiration most profound. Usually beginning on a sombre note, I always concluded with positive and uplifting words. The first poem, 'GONE,' was composed just a fortnight after bereavement and the remainder in the book are more or less in chronological order. In writing these poems I experienced relief from the great emotional pain within, and I hope and pray that as you read them, you will also feel uplifted.

Norman Christie

A moment of helplessness…

"Fear not, for I am with you; Be not dismayed, for I am your God. I will strengthen you, Yes, I will help you, I will uphold you with My righteous right hand."
Isaiah 41:10

Starting back in 2016, I recall a particular day so clearly. My wife Doreen and I were packing, getting ready for our long-awaited holiday to Spain. It was quite a dull day; there was no sunshine and nearly freezing temperatures. Of course, living in Northern Ireland, we were well used to this. Naturally, we were both excited and looking forward to experiencing the warmer climate that lay ahead of us. It was a Wednesday morning, and we were booked to stay for ten days. However, little did I know that as we locked up our family home that day and drove towards our local airport, Belfast International, it was going to be our final trip together. I was blissfully unaware that I would be returning to our home in Belfast alone.

A sudden, painful experience was about to shatter my life completely.

Doreen and I had visited the Spanish Islands a few times. On this occasion, we had chosen to visit Torremolinos in Costa Del Sol. We were so happy to be getting away to spend much-needed relaxation time. Shortly before this holiday, we were part of the Christian Fellowship Tours to Israel, which I had the privilege of leading. In Torremolinos, we were part of a Christian tour group led by a Baptist pastor who was very kind to me when Doreen unexpectedly passed away.

That week, we explored the local zoo, beaches and cafes. In the town, we enjoyed the shopping and were pleasantly surprised one day when a cavalcade of cream-coloured horses with riders in white uniforms rode past. They seemed to be part of a wedding celebration.

We were having a great holiday; unfortunately, things were about to take an awful turn. I remember the sunny Saturday morning that was set to change my life so dramatically. The date is indelibly inscribed on my heart; it was 12th October 2016.

Having greeted friends in the Hotel Don Pablo dining area that morning, this was meant to be our farewell meal in more ways than one; as several hours later, we would be leaving the hotel, bound for our home in Northern Ireland.

Reminiscing with our friends about our holiday and sharing stories of our favourite finds in the local area, we settled down to the breakfast delights of what we would call back home, an 'Ulster' Fry.

However, we had barely finished eating when Doreen complained of feeling hot and dizzy. Trying to figure out if the 'feeling' she was having was to do with the sun or something else, I managed to escort her with some difficulty back to our hotel room. Settling her in our balcony, I thought the fresh air would help her revive and feel better. Unfortunately, it was all in vain, for soon, the symptoms of acute nausea took over.

I knew then she was seriously ill. The pressure was on; Doreen's condition was rapidly deteriorating, so I sent for the local Spanish doctor, who, much to my relief, arrived promptly.

As the lady doctor entered our room, Doreen went into convulsions. It was what I would call, 'a moment of helplessness' - outside my medical knowledge, entering into that moment when time stands still; that moment that many of us wish would never come. The doctor did all she could, including sending for emergency help, but it was all in vain. It was all over; Doreen was pronounced dead.

As I sat in that hotel room, I couldn't quite take in what was happening all around me. Everyone was rushing about, doing their best to take care of the situation; but to them, it was a holidaymaker, another patient; but to me, this was my life partner. Now I was all alone. It is amazing how you can be surrounded by people yet feel so utterly alone. When I thought back over all our years together, I didn't feel ready to live life without Doreen. But my precious wife was now with our Saviour.

I sat for what felt like an eternity. Somehow I started the painful procedure of contacting our loved ones at home and dealing with the hotel management, the undertakers, and the police. A sudden brain haemorrhage had taken Doreen's precious life. I was broken, yet somehow feeling calm.

”

PRAYER

Holy Spirit, who is the Paracletos (One who moves alongside,) fill the empty chair with your Divine Presence. Cause me to rise above the feeling of emptiness into the fullness of your comfort.

GONE

Gone to be with Him above
Gone to walk the courts of love,
Gone from sorrow, sin and shame
Gone to praise His holy name.

Gone to where the children play
Gone to teach and love and stay,
Gone to where the angels sing
Gone to worship Christ the King.

Gone from earthly cares and woe
Gone from fighting with the foe,
Gone where shadows never fall
Gone in answer to His call.

Gone from family now in grief
Gone but hope brings sweet relief,
Gone, we listen for the trumpet sound
Joyful reunions will abound.

The cloak...

"Casting all your care upon Him, for He cares for you."
1 Peter 5:7

The renowned English writer and Puritan preacher, John Bunyan, best remembered for '*The Pilgrim's Progress*,' wrote, *"In times of extremity, one commonly meets with the sweetest experience of the love of God."*

In the last number of years, I have proved the truth of this statement.

Whilst taking time to prayerfully wait upon the Lord, I have frequently been greatly comforted by His unfailing love, enveloping me like a cloak. They say that the first stage of grief is anger, but I was determined not to let anger and bitterness rob me of this moment, of our cherished memories. I often looked back in my mind and studied the life that God allowed me to be joined to - to have that season with, whether short or long. I found that as I looked back, I felt gratitude for the 52 years of blissful married life. It eased the pain of separation and caused me to render my thanks to God.

However, as much as I would love to portray that tears and I never communed, my friend, tears are part of the healing process, and when they come, let them.

I recall one evening being greatly moved with emotion when an elderly gentleman from the Church of Ireland, who had an amazing tenor voice, sang my poem, 'Here' to the tune of a lament composed by the musical group, The Gaithers. The song touched me deeply.

As hard as it is, I believe we need not stumble along life's road in the darkness of death. The One who said, *"I am the Way, the Truth and the Life,"* is always available to help us.

Putting our *'weak hands in the Hand of God is better than a light, and safer than a known way,'* as recited by King George VI.

So many questions arise in our human mind at a time like this. Many times I questioned if I would have to endure this grief for the rest of my life? I can tell you from experience; if we look at death as a loss, grief will endure. But if we look at the life lived (before death), then comfort will come. As Jesus said in Matthew 5:4, *"Blessed are those that mourn: for they shall be comforted."*

Certainly, with the passage of time since my wife passed away, I have found the Lord to be a faithful burden-bearer. God does not call us to forget those whom we have loved and lost, as Scripture states, "In everything give thanks!"

Each day I am thankful to the Lord for Doreen.

"

PRAYER

Dear Father, I believe that you are the Great Shepherd. Just now I walk through the valley of death, but I rest my soul on your eternal promises.

HERE

Here with me in my darkest hour
Here in weakness I feel His power,
Here though broken in grief and pain
Here in Him new strength I gain.

Here in sorrow I come to worship
Here with others bowed in friendship,
Here though my tears like rivers flow
Here upon Him all my love I bestow.

Here as I struggle to think aright
Here am I blest with fresh insight,
Here is His parting at Calvary made plainer
Here do I know His love is greater.

Here afresh I try to understand
Here perceive more of His Divine plan,
Here do I think of those gone before
Rejoicing that sorrow shall be no more.

Cold coffee…

"Have I not commanded you? Be strong and of good courage; do not be afraid, nor be dismayed, for the LORD your God is with you wherever you go."
Joshua 1:9

I recall in my younger years at Everton Primary School in Belfast, during a football match I got kicked in the shin. I was only ten at the time but took the hit well and reacted peacefully. The next day, I was still limping and somewhat in pain. Even though I was in excruciating pain, I knew why and where it had stemmed from… the football match, so I knew I would recover to play another day.

However, what I had never fully appreciated was that severe grief also causes actual physical pain.

The difference is, most of us will not be aware that instead of a shin being kicked, our hearts will be kicked. There is quite a difference. You see, a physio can rub the leg, put ointment on it, even bandage it – but how do you rub or bandage a heart? The damaged heart cannot be seen, but it can definitely be felt! Because of this, we may withdraw from life, from friends or family even, to dull the pain. Some may replace the emptiness with loneliness, isolation, and even in some cases, drink and drugs.

Since Doreen's passing, coming back to our home was never the same. Somehow, and I still wonder why, I would set certain things a particular way, fold things just as Doreen would have. Those small things, or as we say here in Northern Ireland, those *wee* things… all of a sudden, become big things. To me, they are important and, in many ways, crucial.

It was not that I even wanted to bring Doreen back, for who am I to request such? She was with her heavenly Father; she was now in her real home. But I was finding life very hard without her.

In those early days, if something simple happened, such as getting a phone call regarding going for a coffee, it could pose difficulties.

My mind was filled with memories of times in the past when my friend and I met for coffee and chatted. It seems a very minor thing, but I really missed not being able to call out... "I'm away Doreen, I'll not be long!"

I would always keep the appointment. But as we talked about Doreen's life, it would often be difficult to hold back the tears.

Through grief, one gains a fresh appreciation of the Heavenly Father's sufferings, as He saw His Son being torn apart, whipped, and crushed to death with the vicious act of dying on the cross.

Even though a loved one has passed away, we must remember the One who went before us all, suffered and died, so that our loved ones can be united with us one day, through the Blood of our Saviour.

To disengage from the duties and joys of life would be a terrible mistake. Abandoning those coffee meetings with friends would not be helpful in the long run – cold coffee is not God's best for us. Rather, starting to helping others who may be less fortunate than ourselves is a great way forward on the road to recovery. It saves us from falling into the dangerous trap of self-pity, which can lead to our own decline. Mourning must take its course. But in time, and with right actions and attitudes, one can arise from the ashes of death to be a more compassionate, better person. Remember the saying, "Trouble never leaves you where it finds you. It will either make you a 'bitter' person, or a 'better' person."

I recall that even in sunny Spain, as Doreen passed away, the sky turned to rain. In that moment it seemed that even heaven was weeping with me.

There should be no shame in crying.

PRAYER

Father, as I contemplate the sufferings of 'the Man of Sorrows,' I know that He suffered so much more than I can imagine. Because He overcame, I remain confident that I will triumph by His grace.

DISENGAGED

How hard it seems to get involved again,
How easy it would be just to complain!
How strange is the feeling of utter loss,
Until you stand beneath the Cross!

From time to time it seems I am lost,
But yet I've been found at infinite cost,
Knowing the way is already planned,
I rest in faith, at His command.

Touched with the feelings of our infirmities,
Eases the pains of life's uncertainties,
Bold I arise to praise His name,
Thanking God who is still the same.

Engaged in prayer I find relief,
Knowing He hears is my firm belief.
Taking His promises word for word,
Causes my pains to feel absurd.

Taken away...

"Why are you cast down, O my soul? And why are you disquieted within me? Hope in God, for I shall yet praise Him for the help of His countenance."
Psalm 42:5

When Doreen and I were young, a chorus that we sang at the top of our voices was... *"Reach out and touch the Lord as He goes by. You'll find He's not too busy to hear your heart's cry."*

We frequently sang this chorus in our church prayer meetings. Yet even as the years went by, we never forgot those lyrics; they remained true to our hearts. And the Lord has proven himself to me over and over many times throughout the years, that He always has the time to listen to me, He's always there when I need Him most.

It is in these tough times of grief that we learn to lean in closer to the Lord, as Burk Parsons wrote: *"When the Lord takes away, it is so we might cling more closely to what He has already given, namely Himself."*

If only we could grasp the wealth of God's love to us; the abundance of His love, the power of His love to heal, realising His love still shines through our tears, like the sun shining through the rain. He woos us to Himself, especially as we read in the Scriptures in Song of Solomon 2:4, *'He brought me to the banqueting house, and His banner over me was love.'*

Can you find strength to raise that old song? – *"Turn your eyes upon Jesus, Look full in His wonderful face. And the things of earth will grow strangely dim, in the light of His Glory and Grace."*

Such powerful words, yet so hard to sing when you are hurting. We have a choice though, as to how we will react when our circumstances are difficult; we have decisions to make. Just like King David who wrote so many songs unto His God, Scripture tells us after the death of his child, David got up and washed his face,[1] got himself ready and went and praised the Lord. Alternatively, we could decide to be like Queen Victoria after the tragic death of her husband, Albert, when she decided to dress in black and hide away from people for the rest of her days.

Just remember, God is watching on. It is never about what we go through, it is about how we come out. We need to realise that it is possible to grieve the Lord by wallowing daily in death, especially when our dead, believing loved ones, are very much alive in heaven. God forbid that we should thus further grieve the One who died upon the cross for us that we might live eternally.

In my situation, God challenged me with such words as, "How long will you deeply mourn and break my heart?" Like any word from God, He backs it up with Scripture as in 1 Samuel 16:1, *"How long will you mourn…?"* My friend, like Samuel, there must come a time to cross over into a new season.

"

PRAYER

Dear Father, while still remembering, help me to let go of the one you have taken to glory. I realise that in heaven, the joy and happiness you have bestowed is far greater than anything I could imagine.

---

1. 2 Samuel 12.20

ALONE

Alone? - yet surely not alone,
Never forsaken, never remaining in doubt.
Grieved, but He hears my faintest moan,
This I surely know so I need not shout.

Alone? - yet calling out to Him,
Pleading in my thoughts, whispering in my room.
Clearly, He responds to my weak attention,
Showing His Light, dispelling my gloom.

Alone? - yet I discern the Divine Presence,
Sensing His fragrance like a hidden flower.
Feeling that love alone is His sweet essence,
Knowing I prevail through His gracious power.

Alone?- yet praising God for the Holy Paraclete,
Embracing the Spirit in a needy time.
Thankful to God for the messengers I meet,
Angelic maybe, but they help me to shine.

Dealing with moods...

"Finally, brethren, whatever things are true, whatever things are noble, whatever things are just, whatever things are pure, whatever things are lovely, whatever things are of good report, if there is any virtue and if there is anything praiseworthy—meditate on these things."
Philippians 4:8

As children, my brothers and I travelled to play on the beach at Portrush, on the North Coast of Northern Ireland. It was so much fun skimming stones, but in later years, a great amusement park called Barry's opened. They had hobby horses and carousels, but most exciting was their infamous roller coaster called, *'The Big Dipper!'*

I don't think there were too many kids from Northern Ireland who didn't visit those amusements. I remember taking our church youth to The Big Dipper. I recall when it first opened, looking up at the roller coaster. It looked so big from the ground underneath. I thought, *'Wow, this is going to be some ride!'* I never realised that one would have the same fear going up as going down. In between, there were level sections, just enough to try and find one's nerves again. Then it happened all over again.

Like life in general, we will inevitably have good days and bad. We feel we're progressing, then suddenly, something will happen and down again we go, leaving us wondering when this is going to end.

For me, I found after Doreen's death, the afternoons were the most difficult. However, when I was able to collect my grandchildren from school, the joy of their company was indeed uplifting, especially if there was time to take them to a café. As they chatted about school and all their concerns, my negative emotions melted, and my spirits were lifted as my mind focused on them. A smile from children does wonders.

I would leave them to their home and then travel back to mine. Funny that those few minutes with them caused the entrance into my house to not feel as lonely. I knew depression seeks entry into us all, so after a cup of tea and of course a biscuit, off I would go for a walk, or meet up with a friend, work in the garden, pursue a hobby or be distracted with a healthy television programme. It's good to allow choice in your life.

With those ever-changing moods, it is good to remember that even such mighty men of God like Elijah were subject to mood changes. We read in James 5:17 where it refers to this problem in his life, where it says, *"but he prayed."*

Jeremiah the prophet was mightily used by God in proclaiming astounding prophecies which still affect us today. Yet in Jeremiah 20:14 he writes, *"Cursed be the day in which I was born! Let the day not be blessed in which my mother bore me."*

How liberating it is to speak frankly to God and tell Him how you feel!

PRAYER

Dear Father, I feel weak just now, and humbly ask you to strengthen me. I stand upon Your Word, which declares, "I will never leave you nor forsake you."

MOODS

Just now I feel somewhat depressed,
But leaning on Him I find sweet rest.
Turning away from what causes sorrow,
Helps me think of a better tomorrow.

Now and again memories cause pain,
But reaching up to Him new strength I gain.
Pausing to think of heaven and home,
Brings forth the blest songs of richer tone.

Having more time now to contemplate,
Thankful for mercy and in Him leave my fate.
Smiling my best and drying my tears,
Slowly I banish those natural fears.

Turning from mood swings, seeking for peace,
Finding with friends both smiles and release.
Support from my family, who really care,
Eases my burdens and answers my prayer.

Zoom, who?

"Trust in the LORD with all your heart, and lean not on your own understanding."
Proverbs 3:5

Very often, with bereavement, there are feelings of fear. How can I face people alone? How can I sort out my finances, especially if the deceased spouse did just that? How can I shop, do the cooking, etc.? And so the list goes on, depending on one's previous knowledge and experience.

It is amazing what we can do when we try, especially when we ask for God's help and speak to kind friends. Doreen was the computer expert in our home, so when she died, I bought a new iPad and stuck a label on it saying, *"Behold God is my salvation, I will trust and not be afraid."* Isaiah 12:2

This new technology came with a requirement for a whole new level of understanding. The good news was when COVID-19 struck, the iPad became very useful for online transactions, Zoom services and Facebook. For a man in his 80s that didn't really know anything about computers... my confession was: I will trust in the Lord.

I have come to know that God does not want Christians or pastors just to be able to quote Scripture, but we also must allow it to live through us. No matter what age we are, one thing we can all do is learn something new and do something new; after all, Philippians 4:13 states, *"I can do all things through Christ who strengthens me."*

It's only as we address the challenges of life that we prove the validity of these words.

In recent times, I have had to learn about information technology, Zoom and Streamyard. But in this way, online ministries have been developed and I have also enjoyed the experience of authoring new books.

PRAYER

Father, I am so glad that you are Lord of the way I feel. By faith in your great faithfulness, I determine to cast fears aside, and receive your guidance to live a more fulfilling life.

VICTORY

In the battle of life we must overcome,
Overcome through God the Son.
Like intrepid climbers through wind and snow,
Onward and upward we must go.

Suddenly surprised by a stunning shock,
We are forced to stop and quietly take stock.
Devastated and reeling from frightening troubles,
We seek for a way through the dreadful muddles.

Then we remember that He is The Way,
Leaning on Christ is our mainstay.
What shall I say, what shall I do?
Trusting Jesus is the way through.

He is the Mighty Victor who calms the troubled sea,
Calling on Him for mercy is my humble plea.
Suddenly He rises up and takes control,
Now the peace of God is flooding my soul.

Abundance awaits…

"The thief does not come except to steal, and to kill, and to destroy. I have come that they may have life, and that they may have it more abundantly."
John 10:10

You and I could read every book regarding walking on the moon, watch every video about the subject… but until you or I walk on the moon, no book or video will compare to that. Why? Because there is a big difference between learning and doing.

Therefore, have you ever considered that Jesus, who knew no sin, no pain, and no suffering, was 'wholeness' personified on this earth. He could have looked through eternity and observed the pain of the world without acting to alleviate it. But He DID take action - by coming to this sin-ridden earth, becoming sin for us, and bearing our pain.

Here was my Saviour, whom angels worshipped. He left the throne of heaven to feel pain, agony, and death just for you and me.

No matter how difficult it was going to be, Jesus was determined to turn a new page of our lives through His life. A page of sin was washed away through the pain of His suffering on the cross; His death and then resurrection. Accepting Jesus to be Lord of our life releases us from separation from Him when we die.

There will be times in our lives when we must turn over the page and leave the past behind, however difficult it may be to do that. Then, we enter a new chapter with new beginnings as we learn to fulfil God's purpose. Learning to adapt to new beginnings and new things can mean we're often outside our comfort zone. But when that happens, we know we are continuing to grow – and we should live in expectancy of new doors opening for us as we trust in God and ask for His purpose to be fulfilled in our lives.

The Lord says in Isaiah 43:19, *'Behold I will do a new thing; now it shall spring forth; shall ye not know it?'*

May the Lord open our eyes to perceive new ways of serving Him, even enjoying fullness of life. God never offered us a half-life in Him, but an abundant life.

PRAYER

Father, I turn from fretting and rest in your unfailing love. Thank you that your banner over me is love. Through the strength and comfort of your love, I begin to move forward.

MEMORIES

How beautiful the places we went together!
How happy we were whatever the weather!
But now, if I tread those frequented spaces,
My sorrowful soul cries for the missing faces.

Searching the album I soon discover
Photographs, Yes! But where now is mother?
Where indeed is that loving smile?
Just for one embrace, I would run a mile.

How oft when shattered and close to despair,
Her sweet green eyes lifted my care!
The warmth of her touch on my cold hand,
Soothed my fears and helped me to stand.

But yet do I know a far greater love,
Healing my soul from heaven above.
Surpassing whatever a human can do,
The love of Jesus will see me through.

Don't stumble, step...

"To everything there is a season, a time to every purpose under heaven..."
Ecclesiastes 3:1

How naturally do we grow up and accept climatic seasons and changes? The real challenges arise when we face traumatic changes in our lives, such as losing health, employment, or a loved one. However, the underlying fact remains that it is not so much what happens to us, but rather, how we react to our trials, which is of most importance.
The great hymn, "Rock of Ages," was written by Augustus Montague Toplady (1740-78). He was the Vicar of Blagdon in Somersetshire. A sudden storm arose when he was walking in Burrington Combe, a beautiful place, just a few minutes from his home. There was no shelter to be found except in the cleft of a rock by the roadside. He took refuge there until the storm ceased.

He began to think about spiritual matters, and seeing a playing card lying on the ground, he wrote the words of the great hymn, "Rock of Ages," on the back of the playing card. "Rock of Ages! Cleft for me. Let me hide myself in Thee." This playing card with the words of "Rock of Ages" is still kept and treasured in America.

In this season, a stumbling stone can become a stepping stone, leading us to higher and greater things.

In Scripture, our Lord Jesus Christ is described as being like 'a stumbling stone' to some unbelievers, but for those who trust Him, He is the eternal Rock of Ages in Whom we find safe and certain refuge.

Make whatever season you're going through, a stepping stone into treasured memories of the good times, celebrating who God is.

"

PRAYER

Our Father, I look to you to bring to birth new ministries in my life. Thank you for your great patience with me, as I look to You for new ways forward.

CHANGING SEASONS

In the natural we are well aware
Of changing seasons everywhere.
But when it comes to the phases of life,
How suddenly things happen - like the loss of a wife.

Devastated and shocked, elevated or honoured,
We must quickly adjust to the changes as proffered.
Whether in joy, or grieving in pain,
We must by God's grace turn it all to gain.

So even if placed in the sorrow of bereavement,
We may look to God for further achievement.
Groaning as though in the midst of travail,
Bringing to birth we shall yet prevail.

So don't keep thinking that you've had your day,
Just let the Holy Spirit come and have His way.
When the day is lonely and the night fearful,
Bless the Lord and still be cheerful.

The Divine Potter...

"But now, O LORD, You are our Father; we are the clay, and You our potter; and all we are the work of Your hand."
Isaiah 64:8

When tragedies occur in our lives, they frequently bring out the best in us as the Divine Potter shapes and develops new ministries within us.

Since Doreen's passing I have been honoured to have ministered on the mainland United Kingdom and also in Zambia, having visited and taught there in person in 2019, before taking part in online ministry. Now, in your hands, is my first book at 80 years young!

I don't tell you that to boast in me, but in a God that has a path through every obstacle in life, including death. As we read in the Scriptures in Romans 14:8, *"For whether we live, we live unto the Lord; and whether we die, we die unto the Lord: whether we live therefore, or die, we are the Lord's."*

I believe it is important to focus on the celebration of life, not on the loss of life. What would my life have been without Doreen beside me? I could not comprehend.

Today, I thank God that He is the Divine Potter, who can take a life that surrenders to Him and make something beautiful from it. That, He can do for any one of us.

Put your hand into the hand of the Potter and let Him mould you into the next season of your life in Him.

🙶 PRAYER

Dear father, I am conscious, but somewhat confused whilst spinning in circles on the Potter's wheel. Nevertheless, I am glad to feel the joy of the Potter's hands, as He works out His priceless purposes.

THE POTTER'S HOUSE

Made from clay in the beginning,
Beautiful, yet ruined by sinning,
Destined it seemed for eternal damnation,
But the Potter chose amazing redemption.

Merely vessels, vessels of clay,
But God determined to have His way,
The marred vessels seemed hopelessly lost,
But the Potter would buy them at infinite cost.

Thirty pieces of silver was the value placed on Him,
What He? The Lamb of God Who took away our sin?
"The price of blood," they said to buy the potter's field,
Yet the real Potter's field is in the world concealed.

To think how truly blest I am,
A benefactor of God's great plan,
I marvel that He suffered for me,
For the Potter Himself died on the tree.

THE POTTER'S HOUSE cont.

So I proclaim amazing grace,
For He the Potter took my place,
My sin it seemed must be punished,
But the Potter said, "It is finished."

Among God's children I would be,
Worshipping the One, Who died for me.
To be like Him and not another,
For the Potter said; "You are my brother."

Yes now in Him a new creation,
My raptured soul sings of salvation.
To His House I yearn to go,
For the Potter taught it should be so.

In His house I find fulfillment,
Just as I am, needing His treatment,
O the touch of His Hands on this human soul!
For the Potter works and makes me whole.

Standing trial...

"And the Lord, He is the One who goes before you. He will be with you, He will not leave you nor forsake you; do not fear nor be dismayed."
Deuteronomy 31:8

"All stand!" comes the cry in the courtroom; the judge is seated, and then the court begins. In every court case, there are at least two sides, the defence and the opposition. Whether we're one side or the other, we know one thing... at some point, whether we are ready for it or not, there will be an outcome at the end when the gavel hits the sound block.

In life, at the passing of a loved one, we fight with everything we have to stop them being sentenced away from us; then the gavel comes down. As a pastor, I have often sat with people during the final days of their loved ones, hoping and praying that the moment would not come, and yet... it does.

Even knowing death is knocking, no matter how one prepares, when the last breath is taken, shock embraces us. Whether we are waiting in expectation of our loved one's passing, or, like Doreen, it happens 'suddenly;' death is death; it takes from us those we love.

It is during a trial like this that others look on to see if our Christianity is real. How will we react? Will we be bitter or blessed? Are we reflecting on the loss, or the One who said He was the Resurrection and the Life?

The Bible tells the story of how three Hebrew boys walked through the fiery furnace. King Nebuchadnezzar observed a Fourth Man in that furnace. This same Lord has promised to be with us in every circumstance, as recorded in Isaiah 43:1-2, *"But now, thus says the LORD, who created you, O Jacob, And He who formed you, O Israel: "Fear not, for I have redeemed you; I have called you by your name; You are Mine."*

PRAYER

Dear Father, I ask for your enabling grace to thankfully reflect on the past, while praising God for new beginnings.

REFLECTIONS

So many memories emerge from the past,
Some glorious photos make my sky overcast.
Scenes unforgettable may trouble my mind,
Yet celebrations they are of every kind.

Why scenes so positive now feel negative?
But the reality is they were most effective.
Blessings so wonderful all were mine,
Yet celebrations they are of every kind.

Why so cast down when reflections abound?
Cause me to remember happenings profound.
I recall sweet words said at the time,
Yet celebrations they are of every kind.

In eventide now, while the shadows lengthen,
I pause to think of the virtues which strengthen.
Faith, hope and love are what I find,
For celebrations they are of every kind.

First Christmas...

'Be careful for nothing; but in everything by prayer and supplication with thanksgiving let your requests be made known unto God.'
Philippians 4:6

Anniversaries are a difficult thing to go through. One is unsure just how to manoeuvre through the memories and the emotions that come. As well as anniversaries, special days can also be difficult, like the first Christmas after losing a loved one.

Family and friends can feel awkward in knowing what to say as they approach us. Somehow, we must draw a line in the sand... they are only caring. Our response to them should be to care back. On the first few days after Doreen's passing, I was invited, as usual, to join family. I knew it wasn't going to be the same without Doreen's presence there; but on that first year, my family had the delightful idea of inviting me to stay with them for several days over Christmas. This eased the grief greatly as instead of just showing up for a Christmas dinner and returning, it was being about family, relationship, etc, all so much more important than a dinner. It was enough to break the shell that was trying to form around me, and enough to show the family I am okay; that together we'll get through this.

The Bible tells us in Proverbs 10:7, *'The memory of the just is blessed.'* In remembering all such, we are blessed, but we dare not forget the One above all that should be remembered, that He might bring us to God - Jesus Christ.

Christ was slain that His precious blood might redeemed us. But He was also broken that we might be made whole. We read in Isaiah 61:1, *'He came to bind up the broken-hearted.'*

Whatever the nature of the brokenness in our lives, the Lord is well able to bind up those wounds and heal us. Thomas Moore has rightly said, *"Earth has no sorrow which heaven cannot heal."*

Another statement I took to heart when I worked voluntarily for Teen Challenge was, "Jesus Christ, the total cure for the total person."

My friend, Jesus Christ Himself is the total answer for each one of us. Reach out to Him today.

"

PRAYER

Father, help me not to dwell too much in the past. Do not allow me to live in the cemetery, but increasingly enjoy your Presence, and thank you God for my beloved whom your angels have taken home.

THE REDEEMER

Emmanuel, O Emmanuel,
Hark and let His praises swell.
Oh what a moving story!
He came down from the Glory.

He lay, the King in a manger,
To mortal man a wee stranger.
But angels sang and worshipped Him,
Who came to save us from our sin.

He came in His amazing love,
Blest and sealed with the Dove.
How should it be for Him to see,
The perfect way of saving me?

Near His cross I fain would stand,
Thanking God for grace so grand.
And kneeling there at his pierced feet,
Praising Him for the work complete.

A divine encounter...

"I have heard of You by the hearing of the ear,
But now my eye sees You."
Job 42:5

It all happened on a Sunday morning at the Breaking of Bread service, a couple of years after Doreen's departure. I was standing singing some worship songs with the congregation, with my two hands resting upon the pew in front. Suddenly I became conscious of someone standing in front of me in the empty pew and facing me. At first, I did not know who it was, as I could not see anyone. Then I began to realise that this Person was not an angel, but the Lord. He placed two hands upon mine as gently as empty gloves. I did not hear His voice, but I received the impartation of His thoughts, *"I took the best."*

I had never asked the Lord why Doreen was taken in apparent fullness of health. However, Doreen had many gifts, and was an excellent and loving children's worker. Over a period of time, it was conveyed to me that the King wanted her for a ministry to young and aborted children in heaven's nursery. When I look back, Doreen was in her element creating lovely dishes for people. Even when a couple were getting married but had no budget for food, she stepped forward to provide a spread. Previous to this... she cooked for the children in Ballysillan nursery._

Jesus said, *"Suffer the little children to come onto me."* Apart from my own revelation of these things, I was subsequently delighted to hear the testimony of a man on television, who received a heavenly vision in which he saw a nursery for aborted children.

It reminded me of my dad, Richard Christie, a pastor and businessman. He used to say, "*This life is an apprenticeship for the next in heaven.*"

PRAYER

Dear Father, I recall your Word, which says, "Then were the disciples glad when they saw the Lord." I am so glad of those special times of Divine visitation, in whatever form they take. I am hungry for more.

THE VISITOR

He came to me from heaven above,
His hands as gentle as a glove,
Amazed to feel His tender care,
My deepest thoughts before Him bare.

How strange that He should visit me,
This Lovely One I could not see!
Yet in His house so strong His Presence,
Concern and love His very Essence.

His promised Presence He did keep,
To worship Him I fain would seek.
Meeting Him in this startling way
Became a comfort and a stay.

To receive His thoughts, "I took the best,"
Blest my soul imparting rest.
Parting from mum was such a trial,
In the cross content, with self-denial.

Why? . . .

"Call to Me, and I will answer you, and show you great and mighty things, which you do not know."
Jeremiah 33:3

It's okay to ask, "*Why?*"

The Bible refers to us saints as children. And for those of us who have had the blessing of children, then we will have come across those days when the child asks, '*why?*' When that happens, we should never close the child down. Rather, either answer in a way they understand, or say... "I will tell you when you become older."

It's important to know you have the freedom to ask your loving Father, '*why?*'

It is also important to know, He can tell you (in my case He did), or if He does not, you will learn later, the '*why?*' It is God who is one hundred per cent for you as a Father. He seeks only the best for you, just like parents upon the earth.

Even while studying Scripture, there have been times I have asked, '*why?*' For example: Choosing Nazareth to raise Jesus seems a total contradiction for the One whom angels worshipped. This little village at the centre of the rebellious province of Galilee, was far removed from the Glory of the King of Kings and Lord of Lords.

Given a primary school education in Nazareth, was so inferior to the possibility of being taught at the feet of Gamaliel. Brought up by parents in the peasant class, was totally remote from the splendours of heaven. Later, it would be said in John 1:46, *"Can any good thing come out of Nazareth?"*

But Jesus was goodness and wisdom personified, for He was "God manifest in the flesh" (1 Timothy 3:16).

He introduced a set of values which was totally contradictory to the concepts of men. Nevertheless, to such a One, countless sinners, saved by His grace, have bowed the knee and worshipped Christ their King.

"

PRAYER

Dear Father, thank you for the supreme example of servanthood, demonstrated by our Lord Jesus Christ. Help me to follow in His footsteps, despite my obvious failings.

THE NAZARENE

'Altogether lovely' was descriptive of this Man,
He alone could carry such a title fair and grand.
Adored by His mother and worshiped by wise men,
Shepherds spread the word of love beyond our ken.

Not for Him the charisma of vain celebrity,
He chose to walk the talk in His humanity.
Not for Him the passing plaudits of great popularity,
But rather the anointed life of sincere humility.

Not for Him the luxurious life of a celebrated actor,
God working through Him was the preferred factor.
Not for Him the vain applause of the fickle crowd,
But listening to God's words, declaring them aloud.

Not for Him to relish a life of simple ease,
But obedience to the Father, whom He desired to please.
Not for Him this world and its transient fashion,
Serving God above was His big and lasting passion.

Yet can it be, men did not see, His peerless purity,
For laid on Him was all man's sin and gross iniquity.
"Crucify Him, Crucify Him," the bloodthirsty mob did cry,
Seeing Him, the Lamb of God, we can only wonder, why?

What God does, all of God does...

"But the Comforter, which is the Holy Ghost, whom the Father will send in my name, He shall teach you all things, and bring all things to your remembrance, whatsoever I have said unto you."
John 14:26

I was watching our local news a few nights ago. The presenter reported that there had been more deaths than usual from suicide in Northern Ireland in the past twelve months.

How sad it is when people are without hope. Thankfully, as believers, our lives have purpose for all our days here on earth, and hope of eternal life when we pass into the presence of our Lord and Saviour. As followers of Jesus Christ, I am so thankful that we have that hope of heaven to look forward to - that day when we will be reunited with our loved ones. Suicide should never even be contemplated in a believer's life; God does not forsake us when we face challenges such as bereavement. We may go through mourning with pain and tears, but He will ultimately restore us as we look to Him.

As a child of God, there is the Blessed Comforter, the Holy Spirit, to help us. All things work together for us:[2] not just some things, but ALL THINGS. This should inspire us with the hope to look beyond any darkness that surrounds us. Indeed, we are assured of a better tomorrow because of God's grace; the soon return of the Lord Jesus, and our eternal destiny.

It has been rightly said, "What God does, all of God does." How wonderful to think that sinners like us can become born again; redeemed

---

2. Romans 8:28

and indwelt by the Spirit of God, such that our bodies become 'the temples of the Holy Spirit!'

If you are a born-again Christian, God is in you, and you are in Him. Together you have entered a covenant, a partnership, that together you and God will accomplish what He has planned for you. Don't let the devil steal from that plan because of your temporary grief; commit your burdens to the Lord; then you will discover that He is the great burden-bearer.

The old song puts it like this, *"There is One who understands our hearts, Jesus the best friend of all…"*

Let us consider 1 Peter 5:7, *"Cast all your care upon Him; for He cares for you."*

Right now, you can ask the Lord to remove those burdens; you are not alone; He is with you, yesterday, today and tomorrow. Put your hand into His, the One who never lets go… together you and God can do it.

”

PRAYER

Our Father, I give you my burdens, and may Your amazing grace empower me to walk in my todays' in You, and in turn, may I be a witness of the Great Deliverer.

GRACE

Beautiful in its simplicity,
Yet baffling in its complexity.
This love of God so profound,
The story of redemption ground.

How can it be that I should see
His Sovereign way of saving me?
While angels gaze in awesome wonder,
I'm freed from satan, set asunder.

Once deeply stuck in miry clay,
Caught in sin to our dismay.
Christ it was who came to save,
I'm no longer satan's slave.

And so, we joyfully sing and praise,
The One who did our sin erase.
Now altogether in a happier state,
Looking forward to the heavenly gate.

Ever learning...

"When wisdom enters your heart, and knowledge is pleasant to your soul..."
Proverbs 2:10

I believe one of the saddest verses in the Bible is found in 2 Timothy 3:7, referring to these last days! *'Ever learning, and never able to come to the knowledge of the truth.'*

The writings of men depend upon education, natural learning, wisdom and imagination. But the Holy Scriptures are inspired by the all-knowing, all-seeing and all-powerful Spirit of God. There is nothing on earth to surpass the complete canon or measuring stick of Scripture, which has stood the tests of time.

Within the Word of God, we find the answers to all of mankind's problems. Our greatest problem is the sin problem, which no man on earth can resolve. The Bible puts the answer so succinctly in Romans 10:13, *'For whosoever shall call upon the name of the Lord shall be saved.'*

,,
PRAYER

Dear Father, thank you for all that you are teaching me just now. I seem to be on a very steep learning curve. Your patience with me is wonderful. With Job, I can say, *"When he hath tried me I shall come forth like gold."* (Job 23:10).

LEARNING

How abundant in wisdom is God's precious Word!
How different to man's ideas, which at times seem absurd!
How glad I am of the light of God's Spirit!
So freely bestowed and independent of merit.

Reading again that same familiar verse,
Lends new meaning to circumstances perverse,
Uplifted! My soul to new heights does now fly,
Believing the promise, which comes from on high.

Graciously taught, instructed and trained,
Much through the years imparted and gained,
Yet do I feel there is more to learn,
And sharing with others is what I now yearn.

By looking to Him, who is wisdom personified,
We gain more insight of the Saviour crucified.
Seeking wisdom and knowledge from God's perspective,
Delivers from the bondage of being too introspective.

He said, "Learn of me for I am meek and lowly",
Causes our hurried lives to progress more slowly.
By humbly contemplating His perfect life,
We deliver ourselves from a world full of strife.

I'll meet you in the morning...

"...For what is your life? It is even a vapour that appears for a little time..."
James 4:14

How wonderful are the words of Abraham, who was facing the death of his son Isaac at God's command, when he said to his servants, "I and the lad will go yonder and worship, and come again to you!"

Faith like that causes us to rise above adversity and still praise and worship the Lord. The realisation that our God is still the Sovereign Lord in control of all things, enables us to rise above the circumstances, and even in the face of death, worship the Almighty.

The death of a child is particularly tragic. When king David lost his infant son, he said these striking words, *"I shall go to him, but he shall not return to me"* 2 Samuel 12:23. Acceptance and worship can lead to recovery from heart-break.

How striking is the example of the "great woman" in 2 Kings 4, who, having just suffered the death of her son, declared, "It shall be well!"

Sadly, having suffered death (which is the result of the sin of mankind), many become bitter towards God and say such things like, "How could God allow this to happen?" The fact is that God sent His own beloved Son to die, that mankind would be delivered from sin, death, hell and the grave. Consequently, all those who die in the Lord shall live eternally, and we shall meet again. It is not bitterness that we should render to the Lord, but rather thankfulness and worship. 1 Corinthians 15:22, *"For as in Adam all die, even so in Christ shall all be made alive."*

Undoubtedly, death is a most dreadful enemy, but its days are numbered. The Good Lord never intended us to suffer bereavement, so He has done all He can to grant us eternal life and fellowship. When we worship, we are submitting to His sovereign plans, acknowledging that He is Lord, and receiving grace to carry on living victorious Christian lives.

Therefore, for the believer, death is not goodbye, but rather "Cheerio, I'll meet you in the morning."

PRAYER

Dear Father, I thank you as a believer for the ministry of the Holy Spirit in my life. I thank you that He brings comforting Scriptures to my memory, such as, "Because I live you shall live also." And again, I am thankful for 1 Corinthians 15:51-52, "that we shall be changed."

WORSHIP

What a privilege it is to worship Him,
He who saves us from our sin!
Worshipping Him when the path is bright,
Must surely be the believer's delight.

But when it is sad and we've suffered loss,
And the road is steep and heavy the cross.
Worshipping then becomes an effort,
So, we must look to our heavenly Escort.

Afraid, in pain, and dealing with grief,
Then praising the Lord brings sweet relief.
The sacrifice of joy we can ill afford,
Makes Him respond with blest accord.

In adoration of the only worthy One,
Thanking God for His dear Son,
Causes us to rise to realms above,
And afresh we know our God is love.

Standing upon His promises...

"Therefore comfort one another with these words."
1 Thessalonians 4:18

What encouragement there is in the Scripture, Jeremiah 29:11, *"For I know the thoughts that I think towards you, says the Lord, thoughts of peace and not of evil, to give you a future and a hope!"*

Many suggest after bereavement, "One life has been halved because the other half is gone." Similarly, many young people have had their lives severely disadvantaged by the effects of Covid-19, and fear their whole future will be depleted. It is at such times, and in such circumstances, there is always hope in God.

Our Omnipotent God invites us to call upon Him in the time of trouble, and He will deliver us. He also is our Omniscient God, the all-knowing; nothing takes Him by surprise. He knows exactly how to walk you and me out of bereavement and grief and into a new day in Him.

I would encourage you to let go of that fear of stepping forward again by asking for His grace and strength for a new day. As Ephesians 3:20 states, *"Now to Him who is able to do exceedingly abundantly above all that we ask or think..."* Our God can do MORE for us than we can ask or think.

As far as this life is concerned, and the life hereafter, we can stand upon the promise in 1 Corinthians 2:9, *"Eye has not seen, nor ear heard, nor have entered into the heart of man, the things which God has prepared for those who love Him."* Don't waste another moment. Let's pray...

”

PRAYER

Thank you, Father, that sudden-death was no surprise to you, for indeed you know the future. Therefore, help me not to feel guilty as I enter afresh into the further joys of life.

DREAMS

We all have them, night or day,
Some are good, and some dismay,
Like we want our friends to live forever,
Never to lose them, and never to sever.

We make our plans, hoping for the best,
Not knowing some may enter rest,
So when it happens, we feel amazed,
Finding it hard to think, living dazed.

But we must deal with officialdom,
(Some gone before to a better Kingdom).
Their going away has truly been startling,
But we may adjust by simply believing.

Onlookers may wonder and even mock,
But our faith in God delivers from shock,
Realising our times are in God's hands,
Causes us to accept His better plans.

More than pictures...

"Oh come, let us sing to the LORD! Let us shout joyfully to the Rock of our salvation."
Psalm 95:1

Homes that I visited as a pastor had one thing in them that was noticeable ... memories; held in place by pictures. Moving from our large family home when Doreen passed away, to a small apartment, decisions had to be made as to what I would bring with me.

Like all families, Doreen and I had collected picture memories. No matter what room you went into inside our home, memories were on display. But the day came when one cardboard box would hold all the pictures for my new one-bedroom home. Each photograph that would come with me had to be carefully chosen due to limited space. How I came about choosing was quick and straightforward: what pictures meant the most to Doreen and me? Now, in my hallway, hangs those pictures that I go past every morning and evening.

They are the memories that keep me going; they remind me of the rich blessings that God has given me in life; that life in Christ is worth living. And I can say without hesitation that my purpose for living today is as meaningful and rewarding as ever. I have also put my trust in Him for my time remaining on this earth, so I don't live in fear or dread of the future. And I look forward to that glorious day when I'll see Him face to face, to spend eternity in His presence. On that day, I know I'll also be reunited once again with my precious wife and dear friend, my beloved Doreen.

"

PRAYER

Our Father we thank You for the precious visual memories of those who have gone before us. They live forever in our hearts, and because of the death of Your dear Son, we know that soon we will see them again. But best of all, we remember the Lord Jesus. Your Word declares, (1 Corinthians 13:12 NIV), concerning Him, "Now we see what a poor refection as in a mirror; then we shall see face to face." We most sincerely thank you in joyful anticipation. Amen.

PHOTOGRAPHS

How fondly I remember the ones I love!
But now are gone to heaven above.
For me they will never mourn or grieve,
How I wish they never had to leave!

I flick through the photos and see their faces,
And wonder if time our grief erases.
Then I realise this sorrow is common,
All families on earth face the same problem.

For lunch on Sunday there ate fourteen,
But suddenly the table was an empty scene,
Bereaved and saddened by the loss of their mother,
Irreplaceable! There could be no other.

There in the photos we can clearly see,
Surrounded by children, some on her knee.
But now I know, that same sweet love,
Is gathering children in heaven above.

My passion in pictures…

FAMILY: Philip, Pamela, Hilary, Sharon, Doreen and Myself on the occasion of our Golden Wedding anniversary in 2014

MINISTRY: New Church being opened at Ndola, Zambia.

TEACHING: via Zoom

LEARNING: Visit to Israel

To contact the author visit
www.NormanChristie.com

Inspired to write a book?

Contact

Maurice Wylie Media
Inspirational Christian Publisher

Based in Northern Ireland and distributing around the world.

www.MauriceWylieMedia.com